My
First Book of
JAPANESE

FOR MY WIFE,
KELLY, AND FOR
OUR CHILDREN:
DANIEL, IRISA,
LILY, HAZEL, LIAM,
AND GRIFFYN.

**BUSHEL
& PECK
BOOKS**

Published by Bushel & Peck Books, a family-run publishing house in Fresno, California, that believes in uplifting children with the highest standards of art, music, literature, and ideas. Find beautiful books for gifted young minds at www.bushelandpeckbooks.com.

Type set in Providence Sans, Learning Curve, Halewyn, and Chelsea Pro
Artwork licensed from Shutterstock.com.

Bushel & Peck Books is dedicated to fighting illiteracy all over the world. For every book we sell, we donate one to a child in need—book for book. To nominate a school or organization to receive free books, please visit www.bushelandpeckbooks.com.

LCCN: 2022930283
ISBN: 9781638190455

First Edition

Printed in China

10 9 8 7 6 5 4 3

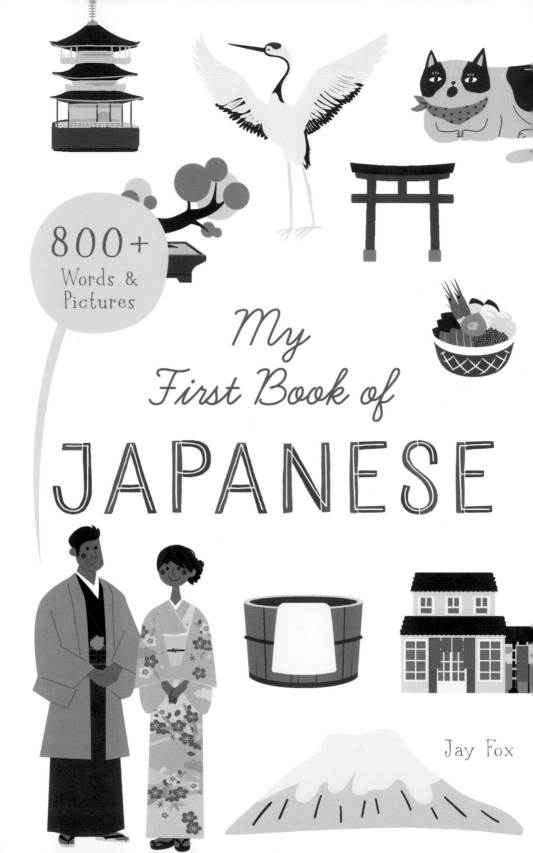

800+
Words &
Pictures

My
First Book of

JAPANESE

Jay Fox

Contents

THE JAPANESE WRITING SYSTEM

VOCABULARY

Good morning!
お早う
おはよう
Ohayou!

THE
JAPANESE
WRITING
SYSTEM

INTRODUCTION

Before we can begin learning how to read Japanese words, we need to discuss the Japanese writing system. The Japanese language is not written with the familiar twenty-six letters of the English alphabet. Instead, the Japanese writing system has three types of characters: *hiragana*, *katakana*, and *kanji*.

Now, you might be asking yourself, "Why do they have *three* types of characters?" Have no fear! The next few pages will explain each type and how they work together.

To get you started, here is an example sentence that uses all three types of characters:

He is eating a banana.
彼はバナナを食べている。
Kare wa banana o tabete iru.

The middle sentence is written in Japanese, with color-coded hiragana, katakana, and kanji (yep, all three get used at once here!). The top line is the English translation (with the same color coding for the translated words or parts of words). The bottom line is written in *romaji* (also color coded), which is a handy way of rewriting Japanese using English letters to make the pronunciation easier. You'll see that used throughout this book.

Ready to decipher each type of character? Onwards!

1 ❯ *Hiragana* ひらがな

Hiragana is a set of forty-six characters—seventy-one characters with *dakuten* (more about that on page 13)—which functions as a kind of alphabet. It is the foundation of the Japanese writing system. Each character is called a *kana*. We will start with the five vowels of Japanese.

VOWELS

あ	い	う	え	お
a	i	u	e	o

As you can see, the five Japanese vowels get transliterated (changed from one writing system to another—in this case, English) as the five vowels of the English alphabet.

Notice that the order of the vowels is different from the standard order in English.

MORAS

Now that we have covered the vowels, it's time to cover the consonants, right? Not so fast! The Japanese writing system doesn't break words down into vowels and consonants. It breaks words down into a special kind of syllable called a *mora*. A mora can be a vowel, or it can be a single consonant followed by a vowel. For example, the の kana sounds like the English word *no*. The き kana sounds like the English word *key*.

Hiragana has a standard order, which is usually displayed in a grid. There are five columns, one for each vowel sound. Each row (after the first) uses a particular consonant.

HIRAGANA CHART

あ a	い i	う u	え e	お o
か ka	き ki	く ku	け ke	こ ko
さ sa	し shi*	す su	せ se	そ so
た ta	ち chi*	つ tsu*	て te	と to
な na	に ni	ぬ nu	ね ne	の no
は ha**	ひ hi	ふ fu*	へ he	ほ ho
ま ma	み mi	む mu	め me	も mo
や ya		ゆ yu		よ yo
ら ra	り ri	る ru	れ re	ろ ro
わ wa				を wo**
		ん n***		

*The し kana is in the s row, but it is pronounced with a *sh* consonant. Other exceptions include ち (*chi*), つ (*tsu*), and ふ (*fu*).
**The は (*ha*) character is sometimes pronounced as *wa* when used as a topic marker in a sentence, and the を (*wo*) character is often pronounced as *o*, without the *w*.
***Notice that the ん character, or *n*, is not followed by a vowel.

HIRAGANA WITH DAKUTEN

が **ga**	ぎ **gi**	ぐ **gu**	げ **ge**	ご **go**
ざ **za**	じ **ji***	ず **zu**	ぜ **ze**	ぞ **zo**
だ **da**	ぢ **ji***	づ **zu***	で **de**	ど **do**
ば **ba**	び **bi**	ぶ **bu**	べ **be**	ぼ **bo**
ぱ **pa**	ぴ **pi**	ぷ **pu**	ぺ **pe**	ぽ **po**

HIRAGANA CONTRACTIONS (WITH AND WITHOUT DAKUTEN)

きゃ **kya**	きゅ **kyu**	きょ **kyo**
しゃ **sha**	しゅ **shu**	しょ **sho**
ちゃ **cha**	ちゅ **chu**	ちょ **cho**
にゃ **nya**	にゅ **nyu**	にょ **nyo**
ひゃ **hya**	ひゅ **hyu**	ひょ **hyo**
みゃ **mya**	みゅ **myu**	みょ **myo**
りゃ **rya**	りゅ **ryu**	りょ **ryo**

ぎゃ **gya**	ぎゅ **gyu**	ぎょ **gyo**
じゃ **ja**	じゅ **ju**	じょ **jo**

びゃ **bya**	びゅ **byu**	びょ **byo**
ぴゃ **pya**	ぴゅ **pyu**	ぴょ **pyo**

*More exceptions to consonant patterns: じ (ji), ぢ (ji), and づ (zu).

2

Pronunciation

Hiragana is based on the sounds of Japanese, so it is also the most useful system for discussing Japanese pronunciation.

VOWELS

- The あ kana, or *a*, is pronounced like the *o* in *pot*, *rock*, etc.
- The い, or *i*, is pronounced like the *ee* in *keep*, *see*, etc.
- The う, or *u*, is pronounced like the *oo* in *loop*, *moo*, etc.
- The え, or *e*, is pronounced like the *e* in *get*, *elephant*, etc.
- The お, or *o*, is pronounced like the *o* in *no*, *tote*, etc.

CONSONANTS

The consonants are pronounced approximately like the English consonants used in the romaji. For example, the romaji for ち is *chi*, which sounds like the first part of *cheese*. The romaji for つ is *tsu*. The *ts* consonant blend appears in English, but usually only at the end of syllables, such as *gets* and *lots*.

THE ん KANA

There is one special kana in hiragana that does not have a vowel sound after the consonant. It is the ん kana, which represents the *n* sound at the end of syllables. It must have a vowel sound before it.

DAKUTEN

We have covered the forty-one main hiragana characters. However, there are more sounds in Japanese. By adding a pair of short diagonal strokes (called *dakuten*) to a kana, you can turn an unvoiced consonant into a voiced consonant. There are four unvoiced consonants that can be changed:

- The *k* turns into a *g*. For example, か (*ka*) turns into が (*ga*)
- The *s* turns into a *z*. For example, す (*su*) turns into ず (*zu*)
- The *t* turns into a *d*. For example, と (*to*) turns into ど (*do*)
- The *h* turns into a *b*. For example, ひ (*hi*) turns into び (*bi*)

Additionally, for the *h* row of kana, we can add a small circle (called *handakuten*) to turn the *h* sound into a *p* sound. For example, へ (*he*) turns into ぺ (*pe*).

CONTRACTED SOUNDS

There are small versions of the や, ゆ, and よ kana, written as や, ゆ, and よ. Note that these are the three kana that start with a *y* in romaji (*ya, yu, yo*). When one of these small kana follows another kana from the い (*i*) column, the *i* sound is contracted (both in writing and when spoken). The two characters become a single mora / syllable. If the contraction starts with the し or ち kana, then both the *i* and the *y* letters are contracted (e.g., *chiyu* becomes *chu*).

DOUBLE VOWELS

When the same vowel sound appears twice in a row, the vowel is pronounced for twice as long as a single vowel.

For example, in the word おおきい (*ookii*), which means

"Go oat!"

"big," the *o* sound at the beginning is doubled, and the *i* sound at the end is doubled as well. That means it takes twice as long to say as the first two syllables of おきなわ (which is "Okinawa," the fifth largest island in Japan).

This can seem a little strange at first, because English doesn't use vowels that are twice as long. One way to get a feel for long vowels is to compare the way *goat* and *go oat* sound (and try not to pause between *go* and *oat*). Another one to try is *heats* and *he eats*.

A note on double vowels: the お vowel is sometimes doubled by adding an う vowel. Similarly, the え vowel is sometimes double by adding an い vowel.

DOUBLE CONSONANTS WITH THE SMALL *TSU*

When a small つ character, written as っ, comes before a kana that starts with a consonant, then the consonant is doubled. Since most consonants can't be spoken for a longer time (for example, the *t* sound is very short), a doubled consonant is usually spoken with a small pause before the consonant. The pause fills in for the extra time of the doubled consonant.

Note: a small っ character will not appear before an n-row kana. If the *n* sound needs to be doubled, then a ん character will appear before the n kana. For example, おんな (*onna*, which means "woman"), has a double *n*.

3

Katakana カタカナ

Cat-a-what now?

Now that we've covered hiragana and pronunciation, it's time to learn katakana. Every hiragana character has a matching katakana character, which sounds exactly the same. (This includes the characters with dakuten and handakuten.) For example, the す (*su*) character can be written in katakana with the ス (*su*) character. The ど (*do*) character can be written in katakana as the ド (*do*) character. One of the unique things about katakana, though, is that there is a way to double vowels by using a long dash. Check out the word for "calendar" in the next paragraph; do you see the ― doubling the vowel?

Katakana is mostly used for foreign loan words. Most loan words in Japanese come from English. For example, the Japanese word for calendar is カレンダー (*karendaa*). However, some words come from other languages. For example, アルバイト (*arubaito*) comes from the German word *arbeit*, which means "work" in English.

Hiragana characters tend to have swoops and curves and loops. However, most katakana characters are made of relatively straight lines meeting at sharp angles. This can sometimes make it easy to tell katakana apart from hiragana. However, sometimes the katakana characters look almost exactly like their hiragana counterparts. For example, へ (*he*) and ヘ (*he*) look almost the same!

In order to make it easier to tell hiragana and katakana apart, we will use a different font in this book for katakana characters. This will help exaggerate the visual differences.

ア a	イ i	ウ u	エ e	オ o
カ ka	キ ki	ク ku	ケ ke	コ ko
サ sa	シ shi*	ス su	セ se	ソ so
タ ta	チ chi*	ツ tsu*	テ te	ト to
ナ na	ニ ni	ヌ nu	ネ ne	ノ no
ハ ha	ヒ hi	フ fu*	ヘ he	ホ Ho
マ ma	ミ mi	ム mu	メ me	モ mo
ヤ ya		ユ yu		ヨ yo
ラ ra	リ ri	ル ru	レ re	ロ ro
ワ wa				ヲ wo*
		ン n*		

*The pronunciations for these katakana characters have the same exceptions and notes as their hiragana versions.

KATAKANA WITH DAKUTEN

ガ ga	ギ gi	グ gu	ケ ge	ゴ go
ザ za	ジ ji*	ズ zu	ゼ ze	ゾ zo
ダ da	ヂ ji*	ヅ zu*	デ de	ド do
バ ba	ビ bi	ブ bu	ベ be	ボ bo
パ pa	ピ pi	プ pu	ペ pe	ポ po

KATAKANA CONTRACTIONS (WITH AND WITHOUT DAKUTEN)

キャ kya	キュ kyu	キョ kyo
シャ sha	シュ shu	ショ sho
チャ cha	チュ chu	チョ cho
ニャ nya	ニュ nyu	ニョ nyo
ヒャ hya	ヒュ hyu	ヒョ hyo
ミャ mya	ミュ myu	ミョ myo
リャ rya	リュ ryu	リョ ryo

ギャ gya	ギュ gyu	ギョ gyo
ジャ ja	ジュ ju	ジョ jo

ビャ bya	ビュ byu	ビョ byo
ピャ pya	ピュ pyu	ピョ pyo

Kanji 漢字

Kanji—I like the sound of that.

Kanji are the Japanese version of Chinese characters (called *hanzi*). Why are kanji based on Chinese characters? Two thousand years ago, Japan did not have its own writing system. However, there were many Japanese scholars, poets, and government officials who were bilingual in Japanese and Chinese. Over a period of nearly a thousand years, a system of writing the Japanese language using Chinese characters was developed.

In modern Japanese writing, a combination of kanji and hiragana is used for writing sentences and even for writing individual words. For example, most verbs in Japanese begin with one or more kanji characters. However, all Japanese verbs end with one or more hiragana characters. In fact, the last character of every Japanese verb will be a hiragana character from the う column. (In other words, the romaji version ends in the letter *u*). For example, the verb "to walk" in Japanese is 歩く. The last character can be written as *ku* in romaji. The first character, 歩, is a kanji character, which is pronounced like ある in this word. Hence, the whole word can be written in hiragana as あるく, or *aruku* in romaji.

TYPES OF KANJI

There are several main types of kanji:

- **Pictographs:** These kanji are a sketch of an object. For example, 木 is a tree, 田 is a rice field, etc.

- **Ideographs:** These kanji are a sketch of an abstract concept. For example, 大 means big, 上 means up, etc.

木
tree

- **Meaning-Meaning Compounds:** These kanji are made by combining the meanings of multiple kanji. For example, if 木 is a tree, then two trees together give a meaning of a grove of trees: 林. What about three trees? A forest: 森. Another example is combining "sun" (日) and "moon" (月), which together make "bright" (明).

- **Meaning-Sound Compounds:** This is the most common type of kanji. These kanji are made by combining two or more characters, where one of the characters is used to indicate how the kanji is pronounced, and the remaining characters give a hint of the meaning. For example, if you take the meaning of the 日 kanji ("sun," "day"), and combine it with the pronunciation of the 寺 kanji (pronounced じ), then you can guess that the kanji 時 has a meaning related to the sun or day and that it might sound like じ. And in fact, 時 means "time" or "hour," and it can be pronounced as じ.

WORDS WITH MULTIPLE KANJI

Most nouns in Japanese are formed from two or more kanji. For example, the kanji 手 means "hand," and the kanji 首 means "neck." If you combine them into 手首, you get the word for *wrist.* If you think about it, this makes sense. Your neck connects your head to your body. Your wrist connects your hand to your arm. Your wrist is a "hand neck."

Another example, which also uses the kanji for "hand," is the word for "letter." 紙 is the kanji for "paper," and 手紙 is the word for a "letter" (a message written by hand on paper).

As you go through this book, see if you can find other examples of where the kanji hint at what the word means.

KYOUIKU KANJI: FIRST-GRADE KANJI

The Japanese education system teaches over 1,000 kanji to elementary school students. These are called 教育漢字 (*kyouiku kanji*), which literally means "education kanji". On the next page, you'll find a chart of all eighty of the kanji taught to first grade children in Japan. All eighty of these kanji appear at least once in this book. See if you can find them all!

Note: In order to keep things a little simpler for you, we've replaced many of the more advanced kanji in the vocabulary section with hiragana instead. The kanji that we did preserve are mostly from the list of kyouiku kanji, especially the first three grade levels, so they're a perfect place to begin!

KANJI READINGS

Most kanji have multiple "readings," which are the way that they can be rewritten in hiragana (which also indicates how they are pronounced). For example, the kanji 日 is pronounced two different ways in the word 日曜日 (にちようび / nichiyoubi), which means Sunday (see page 63).

FIRST-GRADE KANJI

一	one	土	soil	休	rest
二	two	空	sky	先	previous
三	three	田	rice field	夕	evening
四	four	天	heaven, sky	本	book, main
五	five	生	life, birth	文	text
六	six	花	flower	字	character
七	seven	草	grass	学	study
八	eight	虫	insect	校	school
九	nine	犬	dog	村	village
十	ten	人	person	町	town
百	hundred	名	name	森	forest
千	thousand	女	female	正	correct
上	up, above	男	male	水	water
下	down, below	子	child	火	fire
左	left	目	eye	玉	ball
右	right	耳	ear	王	king
中	inside, middle	口	mouth	石	stone
大	large	手	hand	竹	bamboo
小	small	足	foot	糸	thread
月	month, moon	見	see	貝	shellfish
日	day, sun	音	sound	車	vehicle
年	year	力	power	金	gold, money
早	early, fast	気	spirit, air	雨	rain
木	tree, wood	円	yen, circle	赤	red
林	woods	入	enter	青	blue
山	mountain	出	exit	白	white
川	river	立	stand up		

Look for the following tools to help you get the most out of this section:

- 💬 **Example sentences:** See vocabulary in context!

- 💡 **Language tips:** Get extra insight about the meaning or usage of certain words.

- 🌱 **Culture cues:** Learn to love the Japanese culture alongside the language!

VOCABULARY

Greetings

good morning
お早う
おはよう
ohayou

good morning (polite)
お早うございます
おはようございます
ohayou gozaimasu

hello / good day /
good afternoon
こんにちは
konnichiwa

good evening
こんばんは
konbanwa

good night
お休みなさい
おやすみなさい
oyasuminasai

It's nice to meet you. I'm Jay Fox.
はじめまして。フォックスジェイです。
Hajimemashite. Fokkusu Jei desu.

hello / nice to meet you / how do you do?

はじめまして
hajimemashite

 Literally: "For the first time."

bye / see you later
またね
mata ne

I look forward to working with you
よろしくおねがいします
yoroshiku onegaishimasu

 Literally: "Please treat me favorably."

I am _____.
<わたしは> _____ です。
<watashi wa> _____ desu.

 In Japanese, the order of names is reversed. Hence, the family ("last") name comes before the person's given ("first") name. The *watashi wa* is optional, depending on context.

Courtesy

please (give me...)
please (do...for me)
くださ い
kudasai

please
おねがいします
onegaishimasu

thank you /
thanks
ありがとう
arigatou

thank you very much
(polite)
ありがとうございます
arigatou gozaimasu

you're welcome
どういたしまして
douitashimashite

Bowing is customary in Japan when apologizing or expressing thanks.

I'm sorry / my apologies / pardon me
ごめんなさい
gomennasai

excuse me / pardon me
すみません
sumimasen

Is that right? / I see
そうですか
sou desu ka

that's right
そうです
sou desu

no
いいえ
iie

yes (casual)
ええ
ee

yes (formal)
はい
hai

7

People

baby
赤ちゃん
あかちゃん
akachan

person
人
ひと
hito

kid / child
子
こ
ko

child
子ども
こども
kodomo

woman
女の人
おんなのひと
onna no hito

girl
女の子
おんなのこ
onna no ko

adult
大人
おとな
otona

man
男の人
おとこのひと
otoko no hito

boy
男の子
おとこのこ
otoko no ko

💬 Daniel played with a friend.
ダニエルは友達と遊びました。
ダニエルはともだちとあそびました
Danieru wa tomodachi to asobimashita.

people
人々
ひとびと
hitobito

💡 The 々 character acts like a copy of the previous kanji. For example, 人々 becomes 人人.

female
女
おんな
onna

male
男
おとこ
otoko

friendly / gentle
優しい
やさしい
yasashii

friend
友だち
ともだち
tomodachi

8

Personal Pronouns

HELLO
MY NAME IS
山田さん

↖
name
名前
なまえ
namae

Mr./Mrs./Ms./Miss
さん
san

💡 *San is placed after a person's name. For example, Mrs. Yamada would be Yamada-san (山田さん).*

I / me / my
私
わたし
watashi

I / me / my
ぼく
boku

you / your
君
きみ
kimi

you / your
あなた
anata

She is Mrs. Yamada.
彼女は山田さんです。
かのじょはやまださんです。
Kanojo wa Yamada-san desu.

I am Mrs. Yamada.
山田さんです。
やまださんです。
Yamada-san desu.

they / them / their
彼ら
かれら
karera

we / us / our
私たち
わたしたち
watashitachi

everyone / everybody
みなさん
minasan

she / her
彼女
かのじょ
kanojo

he / him / his
彼
かれ
kare

9

Water

ocean
海洋
かいよう
kaiyou

water
水
みず
mizu

waterfall
たき
taki

beach
はま
hama

sand
すな
suna

sea
海
うみ
umi

shore
海岸
かいがん
kaigan

lake
みずうみ
mizuumi

river
川
かわ
kawa

● Do you have a map of Japan?
日本の地図はありますか。
にほんのちずはありますか。
Nihon no chizu wa arimasu ka?

island
島
しま
shima

**archipelago /
island chain**
列島
れっとう
rettou

Sea of Japan
日本海
にほんかい
Nihonkai

A sea of the western Pacific Ocean, between the Asian mainland and the Japanese islands.

the Japanese islands
日本列島
にほんれっとう
Nihonrettou

Honshu
本州
ほんしゅう
Honshuu

The largest island in Japan.

WAKKANAI
SAPPORO
HAKODATE

JAPAN

SENDAI

TOKYO

KYOTO NAGOYA
OSAKA

OKAYAMA

FUKUOKA

KUMAMOTO
KAGOSHIMA

Lake Biwa
びわこ
biwa ko

The largest freshwater lake in Japan. Lake Biwa appears frequently in Japanese literature.

Pacific Ocean
太平洋
たいへいよう
Taiheiyou

Land

land
りく
riku

mountain
山
やま
yama

the world
世界
せかい
sekai

geography
地理
ちり
chiri

region / area
ちいき
chiiki

scenery /
landscape
けしき
keshiki

plain / open field / flat plains
平野
へいや
heiya

🗨 I climbed a mountain yesterday.
昨日山に登った。
きのうやまにのぼった。
Kinou yama ni nobotta.

slope /
incline / hill
さか
saka

Mount Fuji
ふじ山
ふじさん
Fuji-san

💡 The "san" in Fuji-san is not the same "san" used as a suffix for people's names. It comes from 山, meaning "Mount" or "Mt."

stone
石
いし
ishi

rock /
boulder
いわ
iwa

Earth
地球
ちきゅう
chikyuu

soil / dirt /
earth
土
つち
tsuchi

SOIL

ground / soil /
earth
地
ち
chi

Face 顔 かお
kao

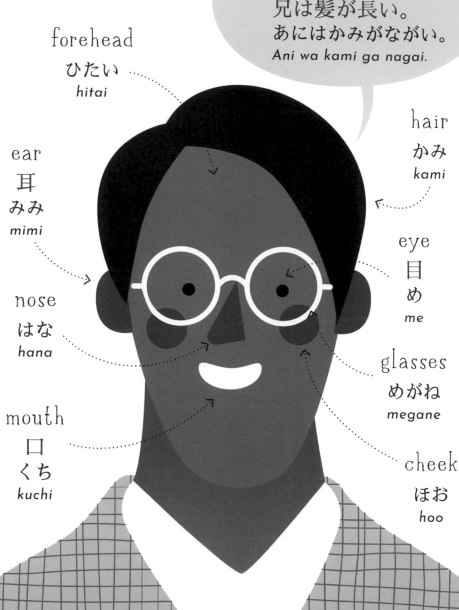

My older brother has long hair.
兄は髪が長い。
あにはかみがながい。
Ani wa kami ga nagai.

forehead
ひたい
hitai

ear
耳
みみ
mimi

nose
はな
hana

mouth
口
くち
kuchi

hair
かみ
kami

eye
目
め
me

glasses
めがね
megane

cheek
ほお
hoo

Body

体
からだ
karada

stature /
height
背
せ
se

wrist
手首
てくび
tekubi

head
あたま
atama

hand
手
て
te

neck
首
くび
kubi

shoulder
かた
kata

finger
ゆび
yubi

arm
うで
ude

heart
心
こころ
kokoro

stomach
お中
おなか
onaka

waist /
lower back
こし
koshi

foot / leg
足
あし
ashi

🗨 I'm taller than my younger
sister.
私は妹より背が高い。
わたしはいもうとよりせがたかい。
Watashi wa imouto yori se ga takai.

Clothing

clothing
服
ふく
fuku

kimono
着物
きもの
kimono

light cotton kimono
ゆかた
yukata

The kimono is the basis of traditional Japanese clothing.

This is typically worn during summer.

This is usually a short jacket and trousers.

💬 Mom is wearing a new kimono.
母は新しい着物を着ています。
はははあたらしいきものをきています。
Haha wa atarashii kimono wo kite imasu.

to wear
着る
きる
kiru

to take off
ぬぐ
nugu

informal summer clothes for men
じん平
じんべい
jinbei

trousers /
pants
ズボン
zubon

coat
コート
kooto

hat / cap /
headwear
ぼうし
boushi

coat / jacket / tunic
上着
あわぎ
uwagi

shoe
くつ
kutsu

shirt
シャツ
shatsu

T-shirt / tee shirt
Tシャツ
ティーシャツ
tii shatsu

underclothing /
underwear
下着
したぎ
shitagi

sock
くつ下
くつした
kutsushita

skirt
スカート
sukaato

14

Colors

色
いろ
iro

 Because "blue" and "green" used to be the same word in Japanese, a green traffic light is still called a "blue light" (青信号 / aoshingou)!

red
赤い
あかい
akai

orange
オレンジ
orenji

yellow
黄色
きいろ〈な〉
kiiro <na>

green
みどり
midori

 Can also refer to greenery, i.e., green vegetation.

blue
青い
あおい
aoi

purple
むらさき
murasaki

💡 Includes other "cool" colors, like blue, green, and gray.

💬 Irisa has brown eyes.

イリサさんは茶色の目をしています。

イリサさんはちゃいろのめをしています。

Irisa-san wa chairo no me wo shiteimasu.

white
白い
しろい
shiroi

black
黒い
くろい
kuroi

gray
はいいろ
hairo

gold
金色
きんいろ
kiniro

silver
銀色
ぎんいろ
giniro

brown
ちゃいろ
chairo

pink
ピンク
pinku

15

My Family

grandma
そぼ
sobo

grandpa
そふ
sofu

mom
母
はは
haha

parents
りょう親
りょうしん
ryoushin

dad
父
ちち
chichi

son
むすこ
musuco

YOU

daughter
むすめ
musume

family
家族
かぞく
kazoku

My dad is a kind person.
父は親切な人です。
ちちはしんせつなひとです。
Chichi wa shinsetsuna hito desu.

aunt
おば
oba

uncle
おじ
oji

sisters
姉妹
しまい
shimai

brothers
兄弟
きょうだい
kyoudai

big
sister
姉
あね
ane

little
sister
妹
いもうと
imouto

big
brother
兄
あに
ani

little
brother
弟
おとうと
otouto

16

Another's Family

grandmother
おばあさん
obaasan

grandfather
おじいさん
ojiisan

mother
お母さん
おかあさん
okaasan

father
お父さん
おとうさん
otousan

invitation / <to> invite
しょうたい 〈する〉
shoutai <suru>

 Certain nouns can be turned into verbs by adding the helper verb "suru." These special nouns will be noted with 〈する〉.

💬 I was invited to my friend's wedding.
友達の結婚式に招待された。
ともだちのけっこんしきにしょうたいされた。
Tomodachi no kekkonshiki ni shoutai sareta.

wedding
けっこんしき
kekkonshiki

marriage /
<to get> married
けっこん〈する〉
kekkon <suru>

aunt
おばさん
obasan

uncle
おじさん
ojisan

older
sister
お姉さん
おねえさん
oneesan

younger
sister
妹さん
いもうとさん
imoutosan

older
brother
お兄さん
おにいさん
oniisan

younger
brother
弟さん
おとうとさん
otoutosan

45

17

Directions

方位
ほうい
houi

magnet
磁石
じしゃく
jishaku

map
地図
ちず
chizu

north
北
きた
kita

compass
方位磁石
ほういじしゃく
houijishaku

Literally:
direction
magnet

west
西
にし
nishi

east
東
ひがし
higashi

south
南
みなみ
minami

far / distant
遠い
とおい
tooi

up / above
上
うえ
ue

down / under
下
した
shita

left
左
ひだり
hidari

right
右
みぎ
migi

near / close
近い
ちかい
chikai

Space

planet
わく星
わくせい
wakusei

space / universe
うちゅう
uchuu

star
星
ほし
hoshi

sky / heaven
天
てん
ten

comet
すい星
すいせい
suisei

> I can see the stars tonight.
> 今夜は星が見える
> こんやはほしがみえる。
> *Konya wa hoshi ga mieru.*

day /
sun /
sunlight
日
ひ
hi

sun
たいよう
taiyou

💡 A more formal way to refer to the sun, as in the center of our solar system.

sun
お日さま
おひさま
ohisama

💡 A cute yet respectful way to refer to the sun (mainly used by children).

air
空気
くうき
kuuki

sky
空
そら
sora

moon
月
つき
tsuki

full moon
まんげつ
mangetsu

19

Weather 天気 てんき
tenki

clear weather
晴れ
はれ
hare

cloud
雲
くも
kumo

lightning / thunder
かみなり
kaminari

storm
あらし
arashi

snow
雪
ゆき
yuki

Notice how the 雲 (cloud) and 雪 (snow) kanji have a shorter, flattened version of the 雨 (rain) kanji on top.

typhoon /
hurricane
台風
たいふう
taifuu

hail
ひょう
hyou

tornado
たつまき
tatsumaki

rainbow
にじ
niji

rain
雨
あめ
ame

wind
風
かぜ
kaze

Plants

植物
しょくぶつ
shokubutsu

tree / wood

木
き
ki

● A large tree stood in the middle of the forest.

森の真ん中に大きい木が立っていた。

もりのまんなかにおおきいきがたっていた。

Mori no mannaka ni ookii ki ga tatte ita.

woods / grove

林
はやし
hayashi

to stand

立つ
たつ
tatsu

grass

草
くさ
kusa

forest

森
もり
mori

bush

やぶ
yabu

leaf
葉っぱ
はっぱ
happa

cherry blossom
桜
さくら
sakura

wisteria
ふじ
fuji

flower
花
はな
hana

bamboo
竹
たけ
take

plum blossom
うめ
ume

rose
ばら
bara

lotus / sacred lotus
はす
hasu

21

Animals

animal
動物
どうぶつ
doubutsu

cow
牛
うし
ushi

cat
猫
ねこ
neko

pig
豚
ぶた
buta

dog
犬
いぬ
inu

monkey
さる
saru

deer
しか
shika

fox
きつね
kistune

big
大きい
おおきい
ookii

small
小さい
ちいさい
chiisai

bear
くま
kuma

polar bear
しろくま
shirokuma

panda
パンダ
panda

raccoon dog
たぬき
tanuki

lion
ライオン
raion

elephant
ぞう
zou

bird
鳥
とり
tori

sparrow
すずめ
suzume

chicken
鶏
にわとり
niwatori

crane
つる
tsuru

crow
からす
karasu

insect
虫
むし
mushi

butterfly
ちょうちょ
choucho

cicada
せみ
semi

fish
魚
さかな
sakana

frog
かえる
kaeru

salmon
さけ
sake

carp
こい
koi

tuna
まぐろ
maguro

turtle /
tortoise
かめ
kame

snake
へび
hebi

22

Seasons

time / period of
an hour
時間
じかん
jikan

the four
seasons
四季
しき
shiki

season
季節
きせつ
kisetsu

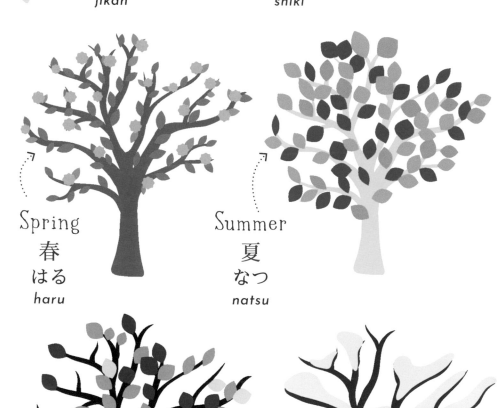

Spring
春
はる
haru

Summer
夏
なつ
natsu

Autumn /
Fall
秋
あき
aki

Winter
冬
ふゆ
fuyu

I love Autumn.
私は秋が大好きです。
わたしはあきがだいすきです。
Watashi wa aki ga daisuki desu.

year
年
とし
toshi

year / counter
for years
年
ねん
nen

this year
今年
ことし
kotoshi

last year
去年
きょねん
kyonen

next year
来年
らいねん
rainen

every year
毎年
まいとし
maitoshi

23

Months

月
げつ
getsu

counter for
months
ヶ月
かげつ
kagetsu

💡 In Japanese, moon (つき) and month (げつ) both use the same kanji (月). Notice that "moon" and "month" are related words in English as well.

January
一月
いちがつ
ichigatsu

1月

February
二月
にがつ
nigatsu

2月

March
三月
さんがつ
sangatsu

3月

April
四月
しがつ
shigatsu

4月

May
五月
ごがつ
gogatsu

5月

June
六月
ろくがつ
rokugatsu

6月

this month	next month	last month	every month
今月	来月	先月	毎月
こんげつ	らいげつ	せんげつ	まいつき
kongetsu	raigetsu	sengetsu	maitsuki

7月

July
七月
しちがつ
shichigatsu

August
八月
はちがつ
hachigatsu

8月

9月

September
九月
くがつ
kugatsu

October
十月
しゅうがつ
juugatsu

10月

11月

November
十一月
しゅういちがつ
juuichigatsu

December
十二月
しゅうにがつ
juunigatsu

12月

24

Days of the Week

Monday	Tuesday
月曜日	火曜日
げつようび	かようび
getsuyoubi	*kayoubi*

calendar
カレンダー
karendaa

week
週
しゅう
shuu

day of the week
曜日
ようび
youbi

this week
今週
こんしゅう
konshuu

next week
来週
らいしゅう
raishuu

last week
先週
せんしゅう
senshuu

every week
毎週
まいしゅう
maishuu

weekday / workday
平日
へいじつ
heijitsu

💡 Fun fact: the kanji 日 can mean "sun" or "day," so it's no surprise that it appears twice in the Japanese word for Sunday!"

1	2
💡 Literally: Moon-day. Compare the English "Monday."	💡 Literally: Fire-day
8	9
15	16
22	23
29	30

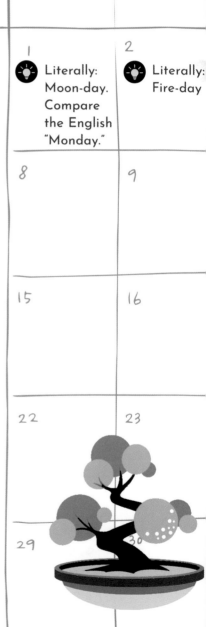

Wednesday	Thursday	Friday	Saturday	Sunday
水曜日	木曜日	金曜日	土曜日	日曜日
すいようび	もくようび	きんようび	どようび	にちようび
suiyoubi	*mokuyoubi*	*kinyoubi*	*doyoubi*	*nichiyoubi*

Literally: Water-day

Literally: Wood-day

Literally: Gold-day

Literally: Earth-day

Literally: Sun-day. Compare the English "Sunday."

💬 Kelly goes to karaoke every Friday.
ケリーは毎週金曜日にカラオケに行く。
ケリーはまいしゅうきんようびにカラオケにいく.
Kerii wa maishuu kinyoubi ni karaoke ni iku.

weekend
週まつ
しゅうまつ
shuumatsu

Time

hour / time
時
じ
ji

11時
じゅういちじ
juuichiji

10時
じゅうじ
juuji

9時
くじ
kuji

morning / AM
午前
ごぜん
gozen

8時
はちじ
hachiji

afternoon / PM
午後
ごご
gogo

7時
しちじ
shichiji

12時
じゅうにじ
juuniji

1時
いちじ
ichiji

2時
にじ
niji

clock /
watch
時計
とけい
tokei

3時
さんじ
sanji

4時
よじ
yoji

5時
ごじ
goji

6時
ろくじ
rokuji

Time of Day

now
今
いま
ima

morning
朝
あさ
asa

noon / midday /
lunchtime
昼
ひる
hiru

evening
夕方
ゆうがた
yuugata

evening /
night
晩
ばん
ban

night /
evening
夜
よる
yoru

midnight
夜中
よなか
yonaka

Lily-chan practices every day.
リリイちゃんは毎日練習しています。
リリイちゃんはまいにちれんしゅうしています。
Ririi-chan wa mainichi renshuu shite imasu.

when? / what time?
いつ
itsu

late / slow
おそい
osoi

yesterday
昨日
きのう
kinou

today
今日
きょう
kyou

tomorrow
明日
あした
ashita

every day
毎日
まいにち
mainichi

every night
毎晩
まいばん
maiban

every morning
毎朝
まいあさ
maiasa

early / fast
早い
はやい
hayai

sometimes
時々
ときどき
tokidoki

27

Countries

country
国
くに
kuni

prime minister
首相
しゅしょう
shushou

Japan
日本
にほん
nihon

America / United States
アメリカ
amerika

suffix indicating a person is from a given country
人
じん
jin

Japanese person
日本人
にほんじん
nihonjin

American person
アメリカ人
アメリカじん
amerikajin

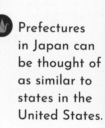
Prefectures in Japan can be thought of as similar to states in the United States.

prefecture
都道府県
とどうふけん
todoufuken

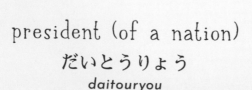

president (of a nation)
だいとうりょう
daitouryou

🗨 There are 47 prefectures in Japan.
日本には47の都道府県があります。
にほんにはよんじゅうななのとどうふけんがあります。

Nihon ni wa yonjuu nana no todoufuken ga arimasu.

👑 Only used for Tokyo.

metropolis
都
と
to

Tokyo Metropolis
東京都
とうきょうと
toukyouto

👑 Only used for Hokkaido.

prefecture
道
どう
dou

Hokkaido
北海道
ほっかいどう
hokkaidou

👑 Only used for Osaka and Kyoto.

(metropolitan) prefecture
府
ふ
fu

Osaka Prefecture
大阪府
おおさかふ
oosakafu

👑 Used for the remaining forty-three prefectures.

prefecture
県
けん
ken

Chiba Prefecture
千葉県
ちばけん
chibaken

28

Urban and Rural

city
都会
とかい
tokai

city
市
し
shi

town
町
まち
machi

zoo
動物園
どうぶつえん
doubutsuen

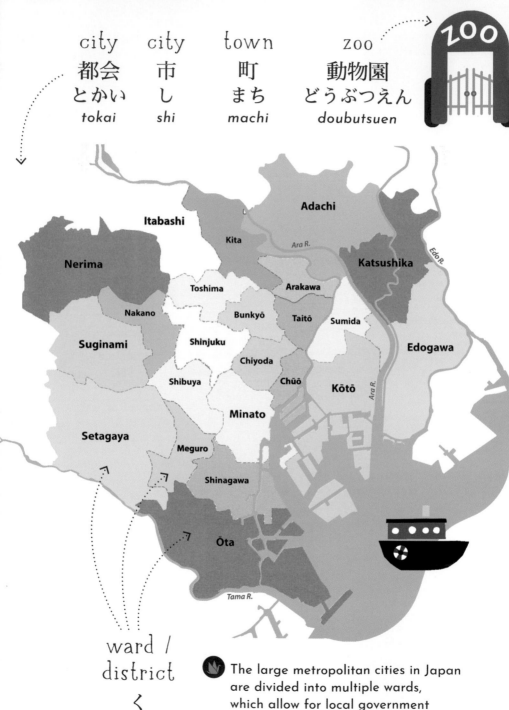

ward /
district
く
ku

The large metropolitan cities in Japan are divided into multiple wards, which allow for local government administration. Tokyo's wards are depicted here.

bank
銀行
ぎんこう
ginkou

hospital
病院
びょういん
byouin

city hall
市やく所
しやくしょ
shiyakusho

art museum
美術館
びじゅつかん
bijutstukan

library
図書館
としょかん
toshokan

field (for growing crops)
畑
はたけ
hatake

village
村
むら
mura

countryside / rural area
田舎
いなか
inaka

71

29

Transportation

to go / to move
行く
いく
iku

to come / to approach
来る
くる
kuru

transportation / traffic
こうつう
koutsuu

bus stop
バスてい
basutei

street
道
みち
michi

signal / traffic light
しんごう
shingou

bus
バス
basu

taxi
タクシー
takushii

car
車
くるま
kuruma

driving / to drive
うんてん〈する〉
unten <suru>

bicycle
自てん車
じてんしゃ
jitensha

ambulance
きゅうきゅう車
きゅうきゅうしゃ
kyuukyuusha

motorcycle
オートバイ
ootobai

fire engine / fire truck
消ぼう車
しょうぼうしゃ
shoubousha

patrol car / police car
パトカー
patokaa

to get on / to board / to take
のる
noru

to get off / to disembark
おりる
oriru

73

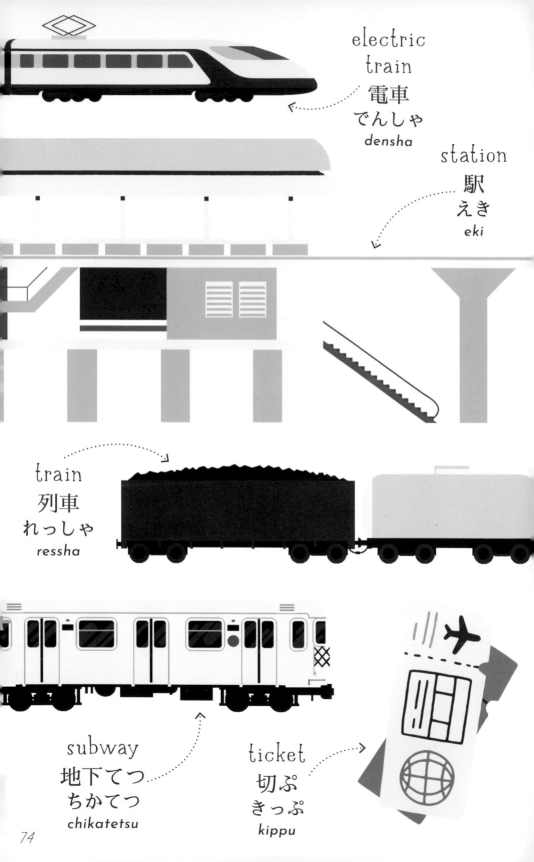

electric
train
電車
でんしゃ
densha

station
駅
えき
eki

train
列車
れっしゃ
ressha

subway
地下てつ
ちかてつ
chikatetsu

ticket
切ぷ
きっぷ
kippu

The Shinkansen, also known
as the "Bullet Train"
新かん線
しんかんせん
shinkansen

The bullet trains can travel up to
300 km/h (186 miles per hour)!

airplane
飛行き
ひこうき
hikouki

airport
空港
くうこう
kuukou

Literally:
Sky
harbor.

to fly
飛ぶ
とぶ
tobu

boat
ふね
fune

harbor
港
みなと
minato

30

Travel

journey / to go
on a journey
旅 〈する〉
たび 〈する〉
tabi <suru>

travel / trip /
to travel
旅行 〈する〉
りょこう 〈する〉
ryokou <suru>

inn (traditional
Japanese-style)
旅館
りょかん
ryokan

to stay
overnight
とまる
tomaru

hotel
ホテル
hoteru

travel
agency
旅行社
りょこうしゃ
ryokousha

reservation / to reserve /
to make a reservation
よやく 〈する〉
yoyaku <suru>

overseas /
abroad
海外
かいがい
kaigai

overseas trip /
travel abroad
海外旅行
かいがいりょこう
kaigairyokou

● Embark on a journey of self-discovery.
自分探しの旅に出る。
じぶんさがしのたびにでる。
Jibunsagashi no tabi ni deru.

hot spring / hot spring resort
おんせん
onsen

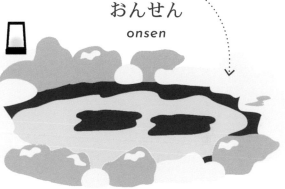

luggage / baggage / package
にもつ
nimotsu

しゅっぱつ

departure / to depart
出ぱつ〈する〉
しゅっぱつ〈する〉
shuppatsu <suru>

to leave / to depart
出る
でる
deru

とうちゃく

arrival / to arrive
とうちゃく〈する〉
touchaku <suru>

to arrive / to reach
着く
つく
tsuku

77

31

Shopping

shop / store / restaurant
店
みせ
mise

how much?
いくら
ikura

to buy
買う
かう
kau

money
お金
おかね
okane

to enter
入る
はいる
hairu

customer / guest
きゃく
kyaku

yen
円
えん
en

dollar
ドル
doru

Japanese currency, very roughly equivalent to a US penny in value, though the exact value fluctuates.

Welcome!
いらっしゃいませ
Irasshaimase!

🌊 This is often used in shops and restaurants.

💡 It might help to think of this as describing a high price or high cost.

cheap / inexpensive
やすい
yasui

tall / high / expensive
高い
たかい
takai

convenience store
コンビニ
konbini

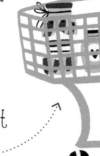

supermarket
スーパー
suupaa

bookstore
本屋
ほんや
hon'ya

bakery / bread store
パン屋
パンや
pan'ya

department store
デパート
depaato

32

Home

💡 いえ and うち are both valid readings of 家 and both mean "house" or "home." いえ is more common, especially when referring to other people's houses. うち is more commonly used when referring to your home, but you will see both variations used.

house / home
家
いえ
ie

home / house
家
うち
uchi

to reside / to live (somewhere)
住む
すむ
sumu

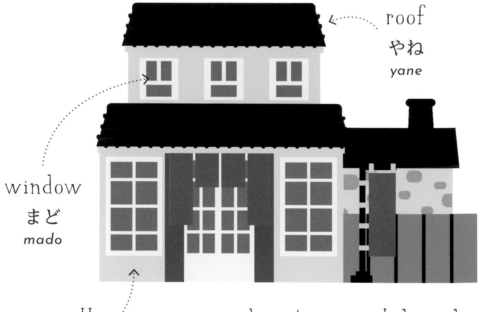

roof
やね
yane

window
まど
mado

wall
かべ
kabe

shoji / paper sliding door
しょうじ
shouji

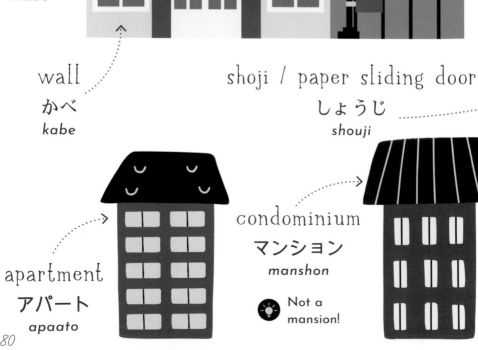

apartment
アパート
apaato

condominium
マンション
manshon

💡 Not a mansion!

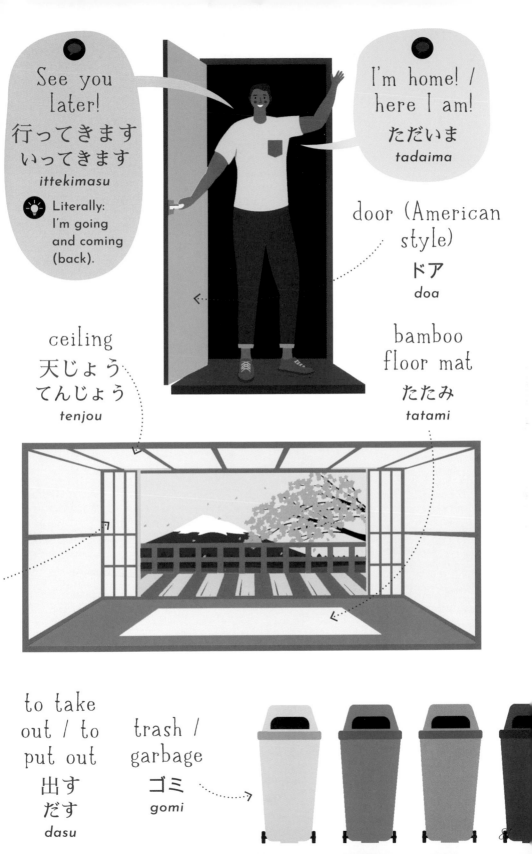

33

Bedroom

bed
ベッド
beddo

**room /
bedroom**
部屋
へや
heya

blanket
もうふ
moufu

futon
ふとん
futon

🏵 A futon is a padded mattress that can be easily folded for storage.

**to lie down /
to go to bed**
ねる
neru

💡 Sleeping is typically implied, but technically, this verb only means to lie down or go to bed.

**closet /
wardrobe**
おし入れ
おしいれ
oshiire

When you leave the room, please turn off the light.
部屋を出るときは、電気を消してください。
へやをでるときは、でんきをけしてください。
Heya wo deru toki wa, denki wo keshite kudasai.

dark /
gloomy
暗い
くらい
kurai

bright /
light / well-
lit
明るい
あかるい
akarui

electricity /
(electric) light
電気
でんき
denki

to sleep
ねむる
nemuru

to awaken /
to wake up
おきる
okiru

turn on /
switch on
点ける
つける
tsukeru

switch
スイッチ
suicchi

mirror
かがみ
kagami

turn off /
extinguish
消す
けす
kesu

Bathroom

washroom / bathroom
お手洗い
おてあらい
oteari

to wash
洗う
あらう
arau

shower
シャワー
shawaa

bath
ふろ
furo

clean / pretty
きれい〈な〉
kirei <na>

bathroom / toilet
トイレ
toire

Traditional Japanese tubs were used for soaking and relaxing, not bathing. Many Japanese homes still have them!

polish / brush (teeth)
みがく
migaku

I brush my teeth every morning.
毎朝歯を磨きます。
まいあさはをみがきます。
Maiasa ha wo migakimasu.

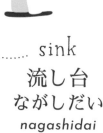

sink
流し台
ながしだい
nagashidai

Kitchen

kitchen
台所
だいどころ
daidokoro

microwave oven
電子レンジ
でんしレンジ
denshirenji

refrigerator
れいぞうこ
reizouko

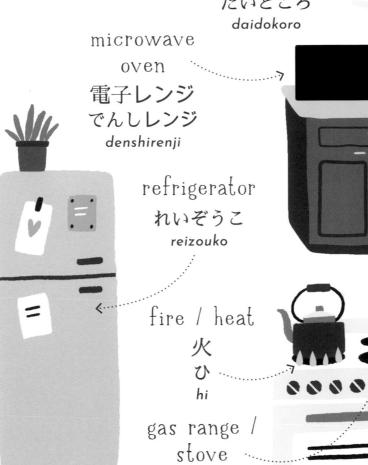

fire / heat
火
ひ
hi

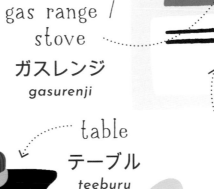

gas range / stove
ガスレンジ
gasurenji

oven
オーブン
oobun

table
テーブル
teeburu

chair
いす
isu

School

school
学校
がっこう
gakkou

kindergarten
ようち園
ようちえん
youchien

elementary school
(grades 1-6)
小学校
しょうがっこう
shougakkou

middle school (grades 7-9)
中学校
ちゅうがっこう
chuugakkou

high school
(grades 10-12)
高校
こうこう
koukou

uniform /
school uniform
せいふく
seifuku

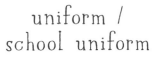

student
学生
がくせい
gakusei

teacher /
instructor /
master
先生
せんせい
sensei

professor /
instructor
きょうじゅ
kyouju

university student
大学生
だいがくせい
daigakusei

university
大学
だいがく
daigaku

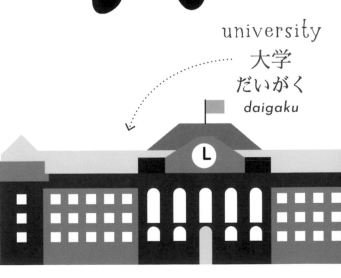

37

Classroom

classroom
教室
きょうしつ
kyoushitsu

to write
書く
かく
kaku

blackboard
こくばん
kokuban

test
テスト
tesuto

火 水 風 土
天 光 愛 連
星 世 大 神
零 使 悪 玉

desk
つくえ
tsukue

pencil
えんぴつ
enpitsu

pen
ペン
pen

paper
紙
かみ
kami

I put the science book in the bag.
かばんに科学の本を入れました。
かばんにかがくのほんをいれました。
Kaban ni kagaku no hon wo iremashite.

to read
読む
よむ
yomu

book
本
ほん
hon

textbook
教科書
きょうかしょ
kyoukasho

bag / satchel
かばん
kaban

💡 For example, a school bag or backpack.

page
ページ
peeji

homework
しゅくだい
shukudai

38

Subjects

education
教育
きょういく
kyouiku

school subject
科目
かもく
kamoku

lesson / class
じゅぎょう
jugyou

language
語
ご
go

Japanese (language)
日本語
にほんご
nihongo

grammar
文ぽう
ぶんぽう
bunpou

Japanese language (school subject for native students)
国語
こくご
kokugo

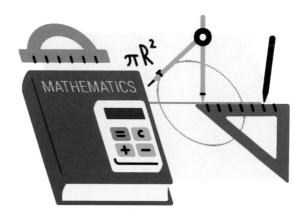

English (language)
英語
えいご
eigo

mathemathics
数学
すうがく
suugaku

💬 Which subject is your favorite?
どの科目が一番好きですか。
どのかもくがいちばんすきですか。
Dono kamoku ga ichiban suki desu ka?

science
科学
かがく
kagaku

history
れきし
rekishi

social
studies
社会
しゃかい
shakai

physical education /
PE / gym class
体育
たいいく
taiiku

39

Learning

to learn
習う
ならう
narau

to teach /
to tell / to
inform
教える
おしえる
oshieru

word
言葉
ことば
kotoba

vocabulary / word
単語
たんご
tango

木

question /
problem
もんだい
mondai

correct / right /
proper
正しい
ただしい
tadashii

to understand /
to become clear
/ to be known
分かる
わかる
wakaru

<to> study
べんきょう 〈する〉
benkyou <suru>

to memorize /
to learn
おぼえる
oboeru

to forget
わすれる
wasureru

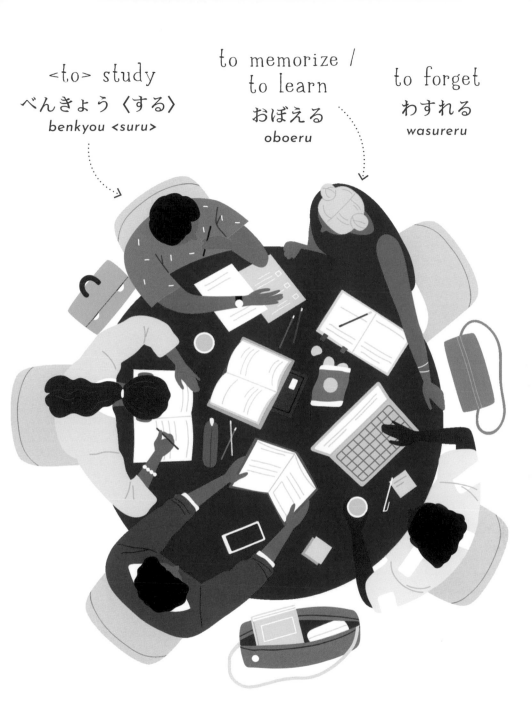

difficult / hard
むずかしい
muzukashii

easy / simple
易しい
やさしい
yasashii

Interestingly, 易しい (easy) and 優しい (friendly) are both written as やさしい in hiragana.

40

Health

health
けんこう
kenkou

injury / to get injured
けが〈する〉
kega <suru>

hurting
いたい
itai

healthy / energetic
元気
げんき
genki

spirit / mind / energy / mood
気
き
ki

illness
病気
びょうき
byouki

okay / safe
だいじょうぶ〈な〉
daijoubu <na>

bone
ほね
hone

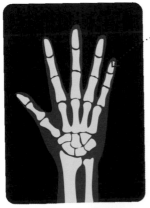

headache
あたまがいたい
atama ga itai

 Literally means "head is hurting."

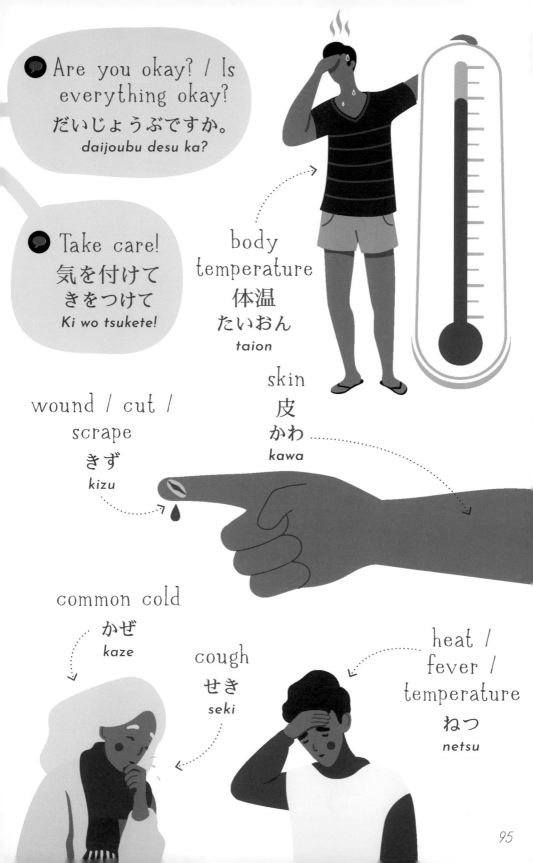

Are you okay? / Is everything okay?
だいじょうぶですか。
daijoubu desu ka?

Take care!
気を付けて
きをつけて
Ki wo tsukete!

body temperature
体温
たいおん
taion

skin
皮
かわ
kawa

wound / cut / scrape
きず
kizu

common cold
かぜ
kaze

cough
せき
seki

heat / fever / temperature
ねつ
netsu

41

Work

work / job / to work

仕事 〈する〉
しごと 〈する〉
shigoto <suru>

to work / to labor

はたらく
hataraku

part-time job / to work part time

アルバイト 〈する〉
arubaito <suru>

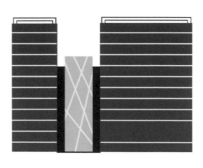

company

会社
かいしゃ
kaisha

meeting room

会ぎ室
かいぎしつ
kaigishitsu

office

事む所
じむしょ
jimusho

member / employee

員
いん
in

office worker / company employee

会社員
かいしゃいん
kaishain

The police officer noticed the thief.
警察官は泥棒に気が付きました。
けいさつかんはどろぼうに気がつきました。
Keisatsukan wa dorobou ni ki ga tsukimashita.

to rest / to take
a day off
休む
やすむ
yasumu

day off /
holiday
休みの日
やすみのひ
yasumi no hi

police
officer
けいさつかん
keisatsukan

lawyer
べんごし
bengoshi

nurse
かんごし
kangoshi

doctor
いしゃ
isha

42

Hobbies

hiking
ハイキング
haikingu

hobby / pastime
しゅ味
しゅみ
shumi

thread /
string /
yarn
糸
いと
ito

to knit
あむ
amu

reading
読書
どくしょ
dokusho

comic
(Japanese
comic books
/ graphic
novels)
まん画
まんが
manga

origami
おり紙
おりがみ
origami

animation
アニメ
anime

movie theater
えい画館
えいがかん
eigakan

movie
えい画
えいが
eiga

game
ゲーム
geemu

💡 For example, a video game, card game, baseball, etc.

fun / enjoyable
楽しい
たのしい
tanoshii

kabuki theater
かぶき
kabuki

🌿 A Japanese traditional form of drama with dance and music.

music
音楽
おんがく
ongaku

to sing
うたう
utau

to blow / to play (a wind instrument)
ふく
fuku

voice
声
こえ
koe

karaoke
カラオケ
karaoke

shakuhachi
しゃくはち
shakuhachi

🌿 A Japanese end-blown flute, traditionally made of bamboo.

piano
ピアノ
piano

43

Sports

sports
スポーツ
supootsu

basketball
バスケットボール
basukettobooru

soccer
さーカー
saakaa

athlete / player
せんしゅ
senshu

Although baseball was invented in the United States, it is a very popular sport in Japan today.

baseball
野球
やきゅう
yakyuu

team
チーム
chiimu

to win
勝つ
かつ
katsu

win / victory
勝ち
かち
kachi

to lose
負ける
まける
makeru

loss / defeat
負け
まけ
make

\<to> exercise
うん動 〈する〉
うんどう 〈する〉
undou \<suru>

to walk
歩く
あるく
aruku

\<to> practice
練習 〈する〉
れんしゅう 〈する〉
renshuu \<suru>

to run
走る
はしる
hashiru

ping pong / table tennis
ピンポン
pinpon

match / game
しあい
shiai

tennis
テニス
tenisu

volleyball
バレーボール
bareebooru

swimming / to swim
水泳 〈する〉
すいえい 〈する〉
suiei \<suru>

to swim
泳ぐ
およぐ
oyogu

44

Martial Arts

budo /
(way of)
martial
arts
武道
ぶどう
budou

🕊 In addition to teaching
techniques for fighting,
budo also gives attention
to the mind and how one
should develop oneself.

stamina /
physical
strength
体力
たいりょく
tairyoku

judo /
gentle way
柔道
じゅうどう
juudou

🕊 Judo is a Japanese
martial art for sport
and self-defense, which
focuses on throwing or
taking down an opponent.
Strikes (punches, kicks,
etc.) are not allowed in
competition, hence the
"gentle way."

jiu jitsu /
yielding art
柔術
じゅうじゅつ
juujutsu

🕊 This Japanese martial
art form focuses on
grappling and wrestling.
A core philosophy in jiu
jitsu is safely redirecting
an opponent's attacks
without injuring them,
hence the "yielding art."

karate /
empty hand
空手
からて
karate

🕊 This Japanese martial
art form does not use
weapons, hence the
"empty hand". It primarily
relies on strikes (punches,
kicks, etc.).

kata / form
型
かた
kata

🐦 In karate, a kata is a detailed sequence of coordinated movements, which is practiced while attempting to maintain perfect form.

sumo wrestler
力士
りきし
rikishi

sumo wrestling
相撲
すもう
sumou

🐦 A traditional form of Japanese wrestling where a rikishi attempts to force his opponent out of the circular ring or to touch the ground with part of his body other than his feet.

kendo
剣道
けんどう
kendou

🐦 Kendo is the "way of the sword," a modern Japanese martial art form of sword-fighting based on traditional swordsmanship.

bamboo sword
竹刀
しない
shinai

🐦 This is used for practice and competition in kendo.

force / strength / ability
力
ちから
chikara

45

Festivals

festival
祭
まつり
matsuri

flower viewing /
to view flowers
花見 〈する〉
はなみ 〈する〉
hanami <suru>

A Japanese traditional custom of enjoying the beauty of flowers during spring. It usually refers to cherry blossoms (桜, sakura), but can also refer to plum blossoms (梅, ume)

summer festival
夏祭り
なつまつり
natsumatsuri

snow festival /
winter festival
雪祭り
ゆきまつり
yukimatsuri

snow
sculpture
雪ぞう
せつぞう
setsuzou

Golden Week
ゴールデンウィーク
goorudenwiiku

Starting April 29th and continuing into early May, Golden Week contains multiple Japanese holidays.

Japanese maple /
autumn colors /
leaves turning red
紅葉
もみじ ・ こうよう
momiji / kouyou

💡 This describes the red,
orange, and yellow
leaves in autumn.

autumn leaf viewing
紅葉がり
もみじがり

momijigari

🍁 The Japanese custom of going to the
forests in late autumn to view the
beautiful autumn leaves.

fireworks
花火
はなび
hanabi

💡 Literally:
flower
fire!

Buddhist temple
てら
tera

Japanese
New Year
正月
しょうがつ
shougatsu

osechi
お節
おせち
osechi

🍁 A traditional food eaten
during New Year's.

Shinto
shrine
じんじゃ
jinja

46

Communication

to speak /
to talk
話す
はなす
hanasu

to say
言う
いう
iu

cell phone
ケイタイ
keitai

make a phone call
電話を掛ける
でんわをかける
denwa wo kakeru

"Hello?"
もしもし
moshi moshi

telephone
電話
でんわ
denwa

radio
ラジオ
rajio

PC
パソコン
pasokon

An abbreviation for パーソナルコンピューター, which means "personal computer."

TV / television
テレビ
terebi

Internet
インターネット
intaanetto

computer
コンピューター
conpyuutaa

post office
ゆうびんきょく
yuubinkyoku

mailbox /
postbox
ポスト
posuto

postcard
葉書
はがき
hagaki

mail /
message
メール
meeru

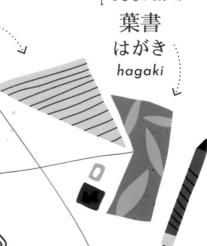

letter
手紙
てがみ
tegami

47

Fairy Tales

story / tale
物語
ものがたり
monogatari

ogre / demon
おに
oni

ghost story
怪談
かいだん
kaidan

goblin / monster
ばけもの
bakemono

king
王
おう
ou

queen
女王
じょおう
joou

prince
王子
おうじ
ouji

the past /
old times
昔
むかし
mukashi

once upon a
time
昔々
むかしむかし
mukashi mukashi

legend / old tale
/ folk tale
昔話
むかしばなし
mukashibanashi

princess
王女
おうじょ
oujo

💡 Specifically, the daughter of the king and queen.

princess
ひめ
hime

💡 A daughter of noble birth (for example, the daughter of a feudal lord or a duke).

katana /
sword
刀
かたな
katana

samurai /
warrior
さむらい
samurai

Japanese
feudal lord
大名
だいみょう
daimyou

 Samurai were military retainers of 大名 (feudal lords) in the Edo period.

48

Meals

cooked rice / meal
ご飯
ごはん
gohan

wheat
こむぎ
komugi

rice
(uncooked)
こめ
kome

"I receive (this meal)."
いただきます
Itadakimasu.

🌸 A polite expression said before meals.

"Thank you for the meal."
ごちそうさまでした
Gochisousama deshita.

🌸 A polite expression said after meals.

dinner
晩ご飯
ばんごはん
bangohan

to eat
食べる
たべる
taberu

breakfast
朝ご飯
あさごはん
asagohan

food
食べ物
たべもの
tabemono

🔥 A traditional Japanese breakfast might include rice, fish, soup, and vegetables.

bento box /
Japanese box lunch
べんとう
bentou

🔥 The food inside a bento box is sometimes made to look like an elaborate work of art or famous cartoon character!

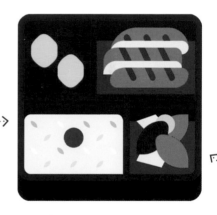

meal / dinner
食事
しょくじ
shokuji

lunch
昼ご飯
ひるごはん
hirugohan

49

Drink

to drink
飲む
のむ
nomu

cafe / coffee
shop / tearoom
きっ茶店
きっさてん
kissaten

green
tea
お茶
おちゃ
ocha

hot water
お湯
おゆ
oyu

black tea
紅茶
こうちゃ
koucha

coffee
コーヒー
koohii

drink /
beverage
飲み物
のみもの
nomimono

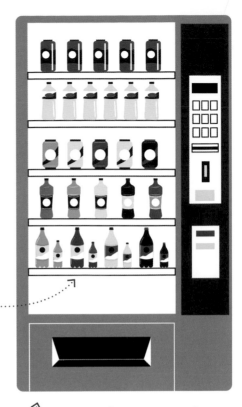

juice / fruit-
flavored soda
ジュース
juusu

vending machine
自動はんばいき
じどうはんばいき
jidouhanbaiki

NEW
Cherry Boom

NEW
PEACH

LEMON

50

Fruits

fruit
くだ物
くだもの
kudamono

apples
りんご
ringo

kaki /
Japanese
persimmon
かき
kaki

Asian pear
なし
nashi

peach
もも
momo

mandarin orange
/ tangerine
みかん
mikan

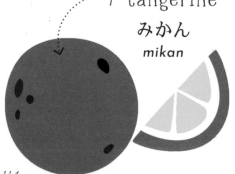

kinkan /
kumquat
きんかん
kinkan

strawberry
いちご
ichigo

grape
ぶどう
budou

fig
いちじく
ichijiku

melon
メロン
meron

watermelon
すいか
suika

banana
バナナ
banana

Japanese plum /
apricot
うめ
ume

51

Vegetables

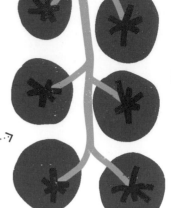

vegetable
野さい
やさい
yasai

carrot
にんじん
ninjin

tomato
トマト
tomato

eggplant
なす
nasu

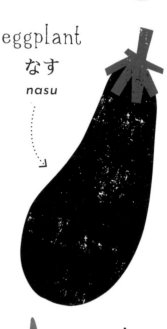

green onion /
spring onion
ねぎ
negi

onion
玉ねぎ
たまねぎ
tamanegi

garlic
ニンニク
ninniku

potato
じゃがいも
jagaimo

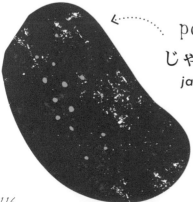

broccoli
ブロッコリー
burokkorii

sweet potato
さつまいも
satsumaimo

green
soybean
えだまめ
edamame

lettuce
レタス
retasu

mushroom
きのこ
kinoko

shiitake
mushroom
しいたけ
shiitake

52

Meat, Dairy, and Eggs

meat
肉
にく
niku

beef
牛肉
ぎゅうにく
gyuuniku

chicken (meat)
鶏肉
とりにく
toriniku

pork
豚肉
ぶたにく
butaniku

fish
魚
さかな
sakana

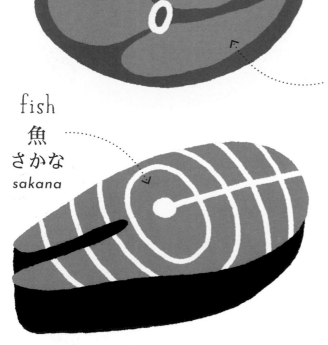

shrimp
えび
ebi

egg
たまご
tamago

shellfish
貝
かい
kai

tofu
とうふ
toufu

cheese
チーズ
chiizu

milk
牛にゅう
ぎゅうにゅう
gyuunyuu

💡 Specifically cow's milk.

milk
ミルク
miruku

💡 Any kind of milk, including non-dairy milks like coconut milk or rice milk.

53

Cooking

to cook / to bake /
to grill / to burn
焼く
やく
yaku

ingredients / materials
ざいりょう
zairyou

to make / to prepare (food)
作る
つくる
tsukuru

to cut
切る
きる
kiru

soy
sauce
しょうゆ
shouyu

cooking / cuisine
/ to cook
料理 〈する〉
りょうり 〈する〉
ryouri <suru>

bowl
茶わん
ちゃわん
chawan

dish /
plate
さら
sara

chopsticks
はし
hashi

cup / glass / tumbler
コップ
koppu

sugar
さとう
satou

knife
ナイフ
naifu

fork
フォーク
fooku

salt
しお
shio

spoon
スプーン
supuun

flavor / taste
**味
いじ**
aji

pepper
こしょう
koshou

recipe
レシピ
reshipi

pot / saucepan
なべ
nabe

cup / coffee cup
カップ
kappu

frying pan / skillet
フライパン
furaipan

kitchen knife / carving knife
ほうちょう
houchou

121

54

Cuisine

restaurant
レストラン
resutoran

sushi shop / sushi restaurant
すし屋
すしや
sushiya

ramen
ラーメン
raamen

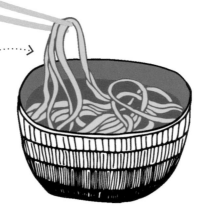

🌸 Chinese-style noodles

delicious
美味しい
おいしい
oishii

sukiyaki
すき焼き
すきやき
sukiyaki

🌸 Thin slices of beef, cooked with vegetables

sushi
すし
sushi

🌸 Raw fish with vinegared rice

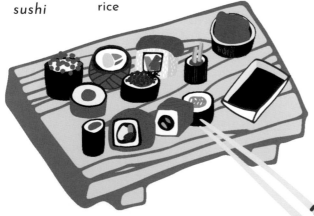

chocolate
チョコレート
chokoreto

sweet
あまい
amai

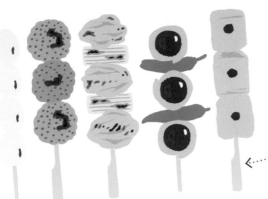

yakitori
焼き鳥
やきとり
yakitori

Chicken pieces grilled on a skewer

teppanyaki
てっぱん焼き
てっぱんやき
teppanyaki

Japanese style of cooking on a large iron griddle

tempura
天ぷら
てんぷら
tempura

Deep-fried vegetables and seafood in a light batter

edible seaweed
のり
nori

Typically in paper-like dry sheets

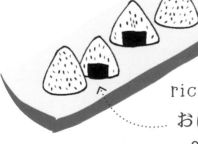

rice ball
おにぎり
onigiri

sashimi
さしみ
sashimi

Sliced raw fish

55

Numbers

digit / numeral
数字
すうじ
suuji

number
番号
ばんごう
bangou

1

one
一
いち
ichi

2

two
二
に
ni

3

three
三
さん
san

5

five
五
ご
go

4

four
四
し・よん
shi / yon

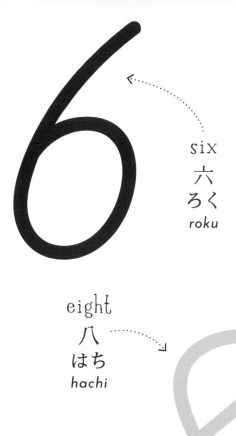

6

six
六
ろく
roku

7

seven
七
しち ・ なな
shichi / nana

eight
八
はち
hachi

8

ten
十
じゅう
juu

nine
九
きゅう ・ く
kyuu / ku

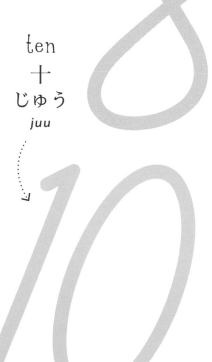

When you see raised dot between two Japanese words, it indicates that either version can be used. For example, on page 124, below the kanji 四, you'll see し ・ よん. This means that the number 四 can be written (and pronounced) two different ways: し (shi) or よん (yon).

56

Bigger Numbers

11	eleven	十一	じゅういち	*juu ichi*
12	twelve	十二	じゅうに	*juu ni*
13	thirteen	十三	じゅうさん	*juu san*
14	fourteen	十四	じゅうよん	*juu yon*
15	fifteen	十五	じゅうご	*juu go*
16	sixteen	十六	じゅうろく	*juu roku*
17	seventeen	十七	じゅうなな	*juu nana*
18	eighteen	十八	じゅうはち	*juu hachi*
19	nineteen	十九	じゅうきゅう	*juu kyuu*
20	twenty	二十	にじゅう	*nijuu*
30	thirty	三十	さんじゅう	*sanjuu*
40	forty	四十	よんじゅう	*yonjuu*
50	fifty	五十	ごじゅう	*gojuu*
60	sixty	六十	ろくじゅう	*rokujuu*
70	seventy	七十	ななじゅう	*nanajuu*
80	eighty	八十	はちじゅう	*hachijuu*
90	ninety	九十	きゅうじゅう	*kyuujuu*
100	hundred	百	ひゃく	*hyaku*
200	two hundred	二百	にひゃく	*nihyaku*
300	three hundred	三百	さんびゃく	*sanbyaku*
400	four hundred	四百	よんひゃく	*yonhyaku*
500	five hundred	五百	ごひゃく	*gohyaku*

600	six hundred	六百	ろっぴゃく	roppyaku
700	seven hundred	七百	ななひゃく	nanahyaku
800	eight hundred	八百	はっぴゃく	happyaku
900	nine hundred	九百	きゅうひゃく	kyuuhyaku
1,000	thousand	千	せん	sen
2,000	two thousand	二千	にせん	nisen
3,000	three thousand	三千	さんぜん	sanzen
4,000	four thousand	四千	よんせん	yonsen
5,000	five thousand	五千	ごせん	gosen
6,000	six thousand	六千	ろくせん	rokusen
7,000	seven thousand	七千	ななせん	nanasen
8,000	eight thousand	八千	はっせん	hassen
9,000	nine thousand	九千	きゅうせん	kyuusen
10,000	ten thousand / one myriad	一万	いちまん	ichiman
20,000	twenty thousand / two myriad	二万	にまん	niman
30,000	thirty thousand / three myriad	三万	さんまん	sanman
40,000	forty thousand / four myriad	四万	よんまん	yonman
50,000	five thousand / five thousand	五万	ごまん	goman
60,000	six thousand / six myriad	六万	ろくまん	rokuman
70,000	seven thousand / seven myriad	七万	ななまん	nanaman
80,000	eight thousand / eight myriad	八万	はちまん	hachiman
90,000	nine thousand / nine myriad	九万	きゅうまん	kyuuman

57

Making Numbers

💡 Japanese numbers are simple to construct. String each place value together, and that's it!

345

three hundred
三百
さんびゃく
sanbyaku

+

forty
四十
よんじゅう
yonjuu

+

five
五
ご
go

three hundred forty-five
三百四十五
さんびゃくよんじゅうご
sanbyaku yonjuu go

Here are some more examples. Can you see the same pattern here?

2,345

two thousand three hundred forty-five
二千三百四十五
にせんさんびゃくよんじゅうご
nisen sanbyaku yonjuu go

12,345

twelve thousand three hundred forty-five
一万二千三百四十五
いちまんにせんさんびゃくよんじゅうご
ichiman nisen sanbyaku yonjuu go

58

Counters

birthday
たんじょう日
たんじょうび
tanjoubi

When saying a specific number of things, Japanese uses special counter words along with the noun being counted. It's similar to how one might say "two cups of flour," not "two flours" in English, only it applies to everything.

1
one (object)
一つ
ひとつ
hitotsu

2
two (objects)
二つ
ふたつ
futatsu

3
three (objects)
三つ
みっつ
mittsu

4
four (objects)
四つ
よっつ
yottsu

5
five (objects)
五つ
いつつ
itsutsu

6
six (objects)
六つ
むっつ
muttsu

7
seven (objects)
七つ
ななつ
nanatsu

8
eight (objects)
八つ
やっつ
yattsu

9
nine (objects)
九つ
ここのつ
kokonotsu

10
ten (objects)
十
とお
too

YEARS OLD

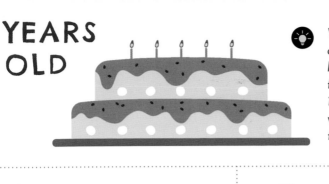

With most Japanese counters, you can use kanji or Arabic numerals for the numbers. Numbers 1-3 tend to use kanji, while larger numbers tend to use Arabic numerals.

1
one year old
一歳 ・ 1歳
いっさい
issai

2
two years old
二歳 ・ 2歳
にさい
nisai

3
three years old
三歳 ・ 3歳
さんさい
sansai

4
four years old
四歳 ・ 4歳
よんさい
yonsai

5
five years old
5歳
ごさい
gosai

6
six years old
6歳
ろくさい
rokusai

7
seven years old
7歳
ななさい
nanasai

8
eight years old
8歳
はっさい
hassai

9
nine years old
9歳
きゅうさい
kyuusai

10
ten years old
10歳
じゅっさい
jussai

PEOPLE

1 one person / alone
一人
ひとり
hitori

2 two people
二人
ふたり
futari

3 three people
三人
さんにん
sannin

4 four people
四人
よにん
yonin

5 five people
五人
ごにん
gonin

6 six people
六人
ろくにん
rokunin

7 seven people
七人
しちにん ・ ななにん
shichinin / nananin

8 eight people
八人
はちにん
hachinin

9 nine people
九人
くにん ・ きゅうにん
kunin / kyuunin

10 ten people
十人
じゅうにん
juunin

OTHER COUNTERS

counter for
small objects
個
こ
ko

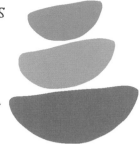

💡 For example:
small rocks or
erasers.

counter for
small animals
匹
ひき
hiki

💡 For example:
pencils or straws.

counter for long
objects and movies
本
ほん
hon

counter for flat objects
枚
まい
mai

counter
for days
日
か ・ にち
ka / nichi

💡 For example: sheets of
paper, slices of bread,
train tickets, or stamps.

counter for machines,
including vehicles
台
だい
dai

💡 For example:
cars, taxis, or
computers.

Word Index

chair / 85

cheap / inexpensive / 79

cheek / 36

cheese / 119

cherry blossom / 53

Chiba Prefecture / 69

chicken / 56

chicken (meat) / 118

child / 28

chocolate / 122

chopsticks / 120

cicada / 56

city / 70

city hall / 71

classroom / 88

clean / pretty / 84

clear weather / 50

clock / watch / 65

closet / wardrobe / 82

clothing / 38

cloud / 50

coat / 39

coat / jacket / tunic / 39

coffee / 113

comet / 48

comic (Japanese comic books / graphic novels) / 98

common cold / 95

company / 96

compass / 46

computer / 107

condominium / 80

convenience store / 79

cooked rice / meal / 110

cooking / cuisine / to cook / 120

correct / right / proper / 92

cough / 95

counter for days / 133

counter for flat objects / 133

counter for long objects and movies / 133

counter for machines, including vehicles / 133

counter for months / 60

counter for small animals / 133

counter for small objects / 133

country / 68

countryside / rural area / 71

cow / 54

crane / 56

crow / 56

cup / coffee cup / 121

cup / glass / tumbler / 121

customer / guest / 78

dad / 42

dark / gloomy / 83

daughter / 42

day off / holiday / 97

day of the week / 62

day / sun / sunlight / 49

December / 61

deer / 54

delicious / 122

department store / 79

departure / to depart / 77

desk / 88

difficult / hard / 93

digit / numeral / 124

dinner / 110

dish / plate / 120

doctor / 97

dog / 54

dollar / 78

door (American style) / 81

down / under / 47

drink / beverage / 113

driving / to drive / 73

ear / 36

early / fast / 67

Earth / 35

east / 46

easy / simple / 93

edible seaweed / 123

education / 90

egg / 119

eggplant / 116

eight / 125

eight (objects) / 130

eight people / 132

eight years old / 131

electricity / (electric) light / 83

electric train / 74

elementary school (grades 1-6) / 86

light cotton kimono / 38

lightning / thunder / 50

lion / 55

little brother / 43

little sister / 43

loss / defeat / 100

lotus / sacred lotus / 53

luggage / baggage / package / 77

lunch / 111

magnet / 46

mailbox / postbox / 107

mail / message / 107

make a phone call / 106

male / 29

man / 28

mandarin orange / tangerine / 114

map / 46

March / 60

marriage / <to get> married / 45

match / game / 101

mathemathics / 90

May / 60

meal / dinner / 111

meat / 118

meeting room / 96

melon / 115

member / employee / 96

metropolis / 69

microwave oven / 85

middle school (grades 7-9) / 86

midnight / 66

milk / 119

mirror / 83

mom / 42

Monday / 62

money / 78

monkey / 54

moon / 49

morning / 66

morning / AM / 64

mother / 44

motorcycle / 73

mountain / 34

Mount Fuji / 35

mouth / 36

movie / 98

movie theater / 98

Mr./Mrs./Ms./Miss / 30

mushroom / 117

music / 99

name / 30

near / close / 47

neck / 37

next month / 61

next week / 62

next year / 59

night / evening / 66

nine / 125

nine (objects) / 130

nine people / 132

nine years old / 131

no / 27

noon / midday / lunchtime / 66

north / 46

nose / 36

November / 61

now / 66

number / 124

nurse / 97

ocean / 32

October / 61

office / 96

office worker / company employee / 96

ogre / demon / 108

okay / safe / 94

older brother / 45

older sister / 45

once upon a time / 109

one / 124

one (object) / 130

one person / alone / 132

one year old / 131

onion / 116

orange / 40

origami / 98

Osaka Prefecture / 69

osechi / 105

oven / 85

overseas / abroad / 76

overseas trip / travel abroad / 76

Pacific Ocean / 33

page / 89

panda / 55

paper / 88

parents / 42

part-time job / to work part time / 96

sisters / 43

six / 125

six (objects) / 130

six people / 132

six years old / 131

skin / 95

skirt / 39

sky / 49

sky / heaven / 48

slope / incline / hill / 35

small / 55

snake / 57

snow / 50

snow festival / winter festival / 104

snow sculpture / 104

soccer / 100

social studies / 91

sock / 39

soil / dirt / earth / 35

sometimes / 67

son / 42

south / 46

soy sauce / 120

space / universe / 48

sparrow / 56

spirit / mind / energy / mood / 94

spoon / 121

sports / 100

Spring / 58

stamina / physical strength / 102

star / 48

station / 74

stature / height / 37

stomach / 37

stone / 35

storm / 50

story / tale / 108

strawberry / 115

street / 72

student / 87

subway / 74

suffix indicating a person is from a given country / 68

sugar / 121

sukiyaki / 122

Summer / 58

summer festival / 104

sumo wrestler / 103

sumo wrestling / 103

sun / 49

Sunday / 63

supermarket / 79

sushi / 122

sushi shop / sushi restaurant / 122

sweet / 122

sweet potato / 117

swimming / to swim / 101

switch / 83

table / 85

Take care! / 95

tall / high / expensive / 79

taxi / 72

teacher / instructor / master / 87

team / 100

telephone / 106

tempura / 123

ten / 125

tennis / 101

ten (objects) / 130

ten people / 132

ten years old / 131

teppanyaki / 123

test / 88

textbook / 89

"Thank you for the meal." / 110

thank you / thanks / 26

thank you very much (polite) / 26

that's right / 27

the four seasons / 58

the Japanese islands / 33

the past / old times / 109

The Shinkansen, also known as the "Bullet Train" / 75

the world / 34

they / them / their / 31

this month / 61

this week / 62

this year / 59

thread / string / yarn / 98

three / 124

three hundred forty-five / 128

three (objects) / 130

three people / 132

three years old / 131

Thursday / 63

ticket / 74

time / period of an hour / 58

to arrive / to reach / 77

to awaken / to wake up / 83

to blow / to play (a wind instrument) / 99

to buy / 78

to come / to approach / 72

to cook / to bake / to grill / to burn / 120

to cut / 120

today / 67

to drink / 112

to eat / 110

to enter / 78

to fly / 75

to forget / 93

tofu / 119

to get off / to disembark / 73

to get on / to board / to take / 73

to go / to move / 72

to knit / 98

Tokyo Metropolis / 69

to learn / 92

to leave / to depart / 77

to lie down / to go to bed / 82

to lose / 100

to make / to prepare

(food) / 120

tomato / 116

to memorize / to learn / 93

tomorrow / 67

to read / 89

to reside / to live (somewhere) / 80

to rest / to take a day off / 97

tornado / 51

to run / 101

to say / 106

to sing / 99

to sleep / 83

to speak / to talk / 106

to stand / 52

to stay overnight / 76

to swim / 101

to take off / 38

to take out / to put out / 81

to teach / to tell / to inform / 92

to understand / to become clear / to be known / 92

to walk / 101

to wash / 84

to wear / 38

to win / 100

town / 70

to work / to labor / 96

to write / 88

train / 74

transportation / traffic

/ 72

trash / garbage / 81

travel agency / 76

travel / trip / to travel / 76

tree / wood / 52

trousers / pants / 39

T-shirt / tee shirt / 39

Tuesday / 62

tuna / 57

turn off / extinguish / 83

turn on / switch on / 83

turtle / tortoise / 57

TV / television / 107

two / 124

two (objects) / 130

two people / 132

two years old / 131

typhoon / hurricane / 51

uncle / 43

uncle / 45

underclothing / underwear / 39

uniform / school uniform / 87

university / 87

university student / 87

up / above / 47

vegetable / 116

vending machine / 113

village / 71

vocabulary / word / 92

voice / 99

volleyball / 101

waist /

ABOUT THE AUTHOR

Jay Fox grew up in San Jose, California, in the heart of Silicon Valley. Surrounded by cultural and ethnic diversity, Jay took an early interest in learning languages. His two favorite foreign languages are German and Japanese, and he has invested years of study in both. Over the years, he has also dabbled in Spanish, Russian, French, and Hebrew.

As luck would have it, Jay managed to go to Germany in high school as part of a foreign exchange program, during which time he was able to visit eight countries in Europe. He looks forward to being able to travel to Japan someday.

Jay currently lives in Fresno, California, with his wife and six children. When he isn't working or studying foreign languages, he enjoys playing games and watching anime with his children.

ABOUT BUSHEL & PECK BOOKS

Bushel & Peck Books is a children's publishing house with a special mission. Through our Book-for-Book Promise™, we donate one book to kids in need for every book we sell. Our beautiful books are given to kids through schools, libraries, local neighborhoods, shelters, nonprofits, and also to many selfless organizations that are working hard to make a difference. So thank you for purchasing this book! Because of you, another book will make its way into the hands of a child who needs it most.

NOMINATE A SCHOOL OR ORGANIZATION TO RECEIVE FREE BOOKS

Do you know a school, library, or organization that could use some free books for their kids? We'd love to help! Please fill out the nomination form on our website, and we'll do everything we can to make something happen.

www.bushelandpeckbooks.com/pages/
nominate-a-school-or-organization

If you liked this book, please leave a review online at your favorite retailer. Honest reviews spread the word about Bushel & Peck—and help us make better books, too!